"By associating with the cat, one only
risks becoming richer."
— Colette
The Tendrils of the Vine

ISBN 0-89954-198-4

First edition, 1990, The Laughing Academy Press,
Columbus, Ohio 43202

Manufactured in the U.S.A.
Printed and bound by Antioch Publishing Company,
Yellow Springs, Ohio 45387

ONLY TWO
(SEEMS LIKE MORE)

Susan Sturgill

Antioch Publishing Company
Yellow Springs, Ohio 45387

For Claire

The Essence of Felinicity

...to have dominion over the humans.

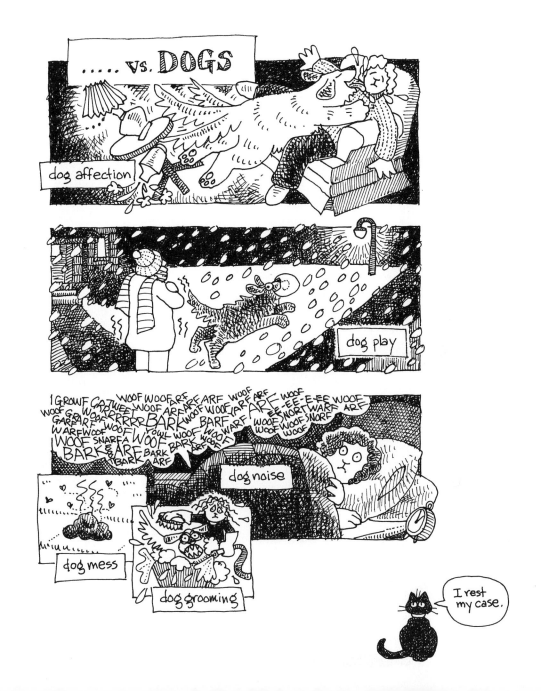

Butch Breaks His Diet

Pavlov's Cats

it's a bird! it's a plane!
IT'S SUPPERMAN!

Refrigerator Magnets

Cats do not approve of smoking

Cats enjoy the occasional evening of mindless entertainment.....

.... but they prefer an educational nature program.

Cats like to stay on top of current events

Cats hate cleaning

.... because it disturbs the arrangement of their toys.

Family Outing

Winter Vacation

The morning grooming ritual

Cats do not understand the appeal of full immersion bathing.

Cats Like to Help

A CATALOG OF HOME OFFICE ACCESSORIES

Couch Potato and Meatloaves

Tunafish
your favorite
dish...

An exercise
partner is a BIG help....

Cats become seriously concerned when they see
otherwise sane people take to exercise equipment.

Cats like to make houseguests feel welcome ....

Morning Thunder

Cats Just Want to Have Fun

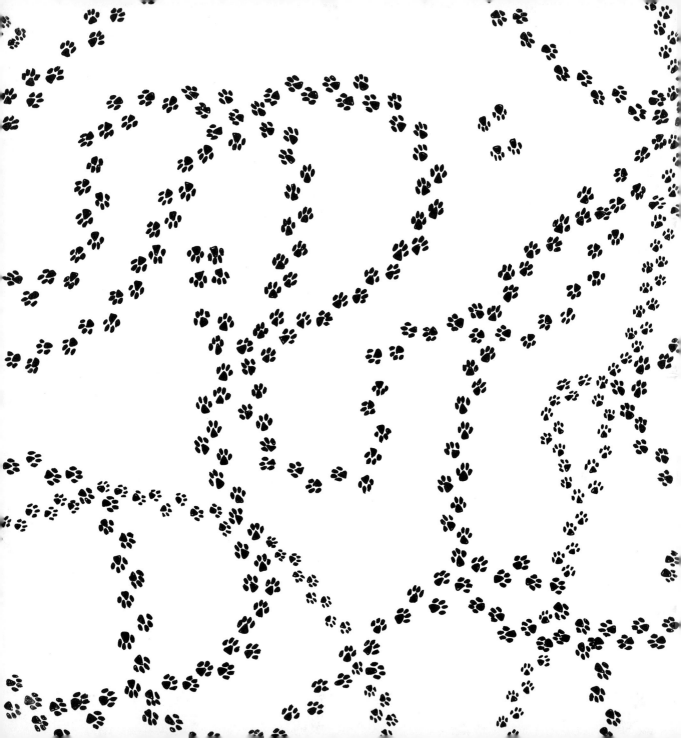